The Joy of
Italian Melodies

**Best-loved songs, arias and folk tunes in
easy piano arrangements.
Selected and arranged by Denes Agay and Frank Metis.**

Cover design by Mike Bell Design, London

Order No. YK21801
US International Standard Book Number: 0.8256.8099.9
UK International Standard Book Number: 0.7119.6758.X

Exclusive Distributors:
Contact us:
Hal Leonard
7777 West Bluemound Road,
Milwaukee, WI 53213
Email: info@halleonard.com

In Europe, contact:
Hal Leonard Europe Limited
42 Wigmore Street, Marylebone,
London WIU 2RY
Email: info@halleonardeurope.com

In Australia, contact:
Hal Leonard Australia Pty. Ltd.
4 Lentara Court, Cheltenham, Victoria 9132, Australia
Email: info@halleonard.com.au

Printed in the EU

Yorktown Music Press, Inc.

Contents

Tiritomba

Folk Song

Ciribiribin

A. Pestalozza

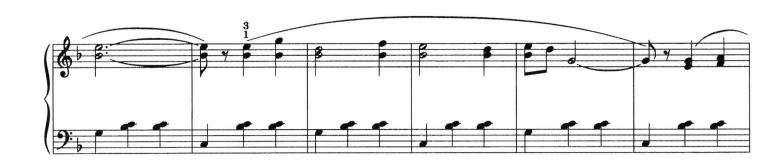

Caro Nome

from "Rigoletto"

Giuseppe Verdi

La Donna è Mobile

from "Rigoletto"

Giuseppe Verdi

Vesti la Giubba

from "Pagliacci"

Ruggiero Leoncavallo

Come Back to Sorrento

Torna a Surriento

Ernesto de Curtis

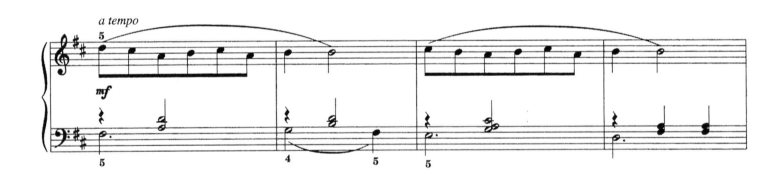

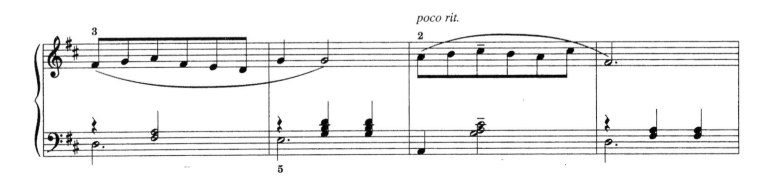

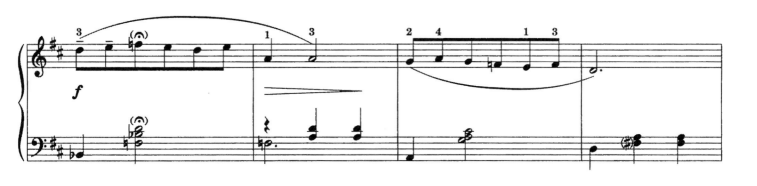

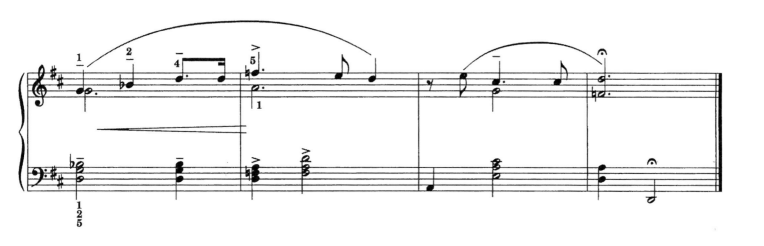

Ah, Fors' è Lui

from "La Traviata"

Giuseppe Verdi

Addio del Passato

from "La Traviata"

Giuseppe Verdi

Moderately slow, with feeling

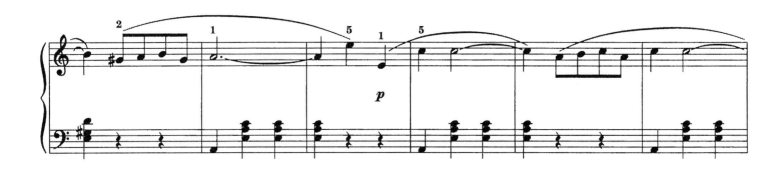

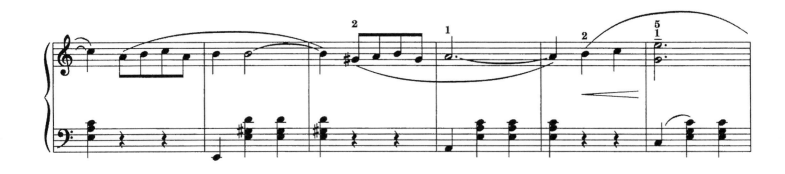

Mattinata

Ruggiero Leoncavallo

Musetta's Waltz

from "La Bohème"

Giacomo Puccini

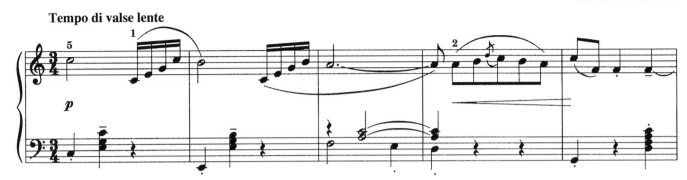

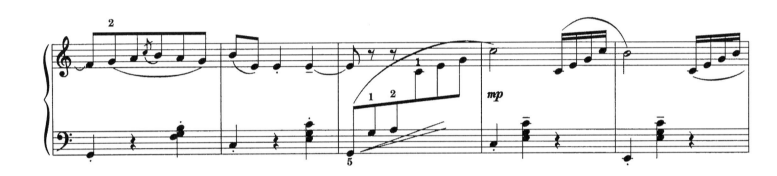

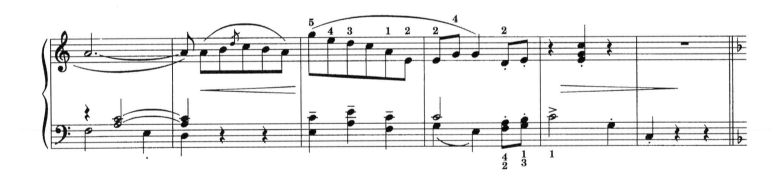

Celeste Aïda

from "Aïda"

Giuseppe Verdi

Vissi d'Arte

from "Tosca"

Giacomo Puccini

E Lucevan le Stelle

from "Tosca"

Giacomo Puccini

O Sole Mio

Eduardo di Capua

Santa Lucia

Folk Song

Serenata

Rimpianto

Enrico Toselli

Funiculi, Funicula

Luigi Denza

Vieni sul Mar

Traditional

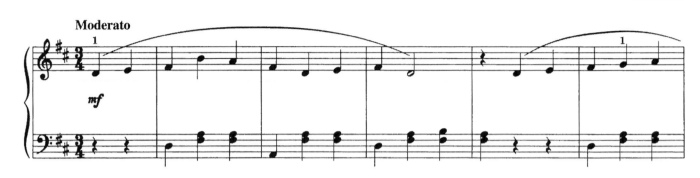

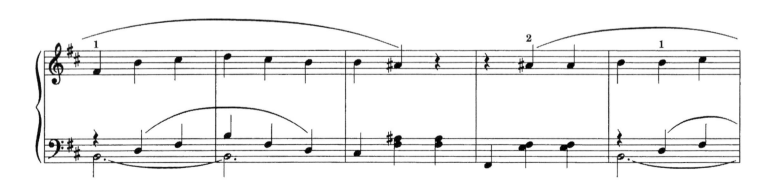

Piacer d'Amor

Plaisir d'Amour

Giovanni Martini

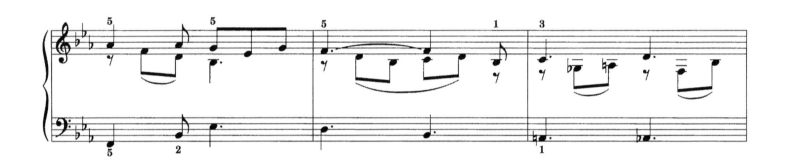

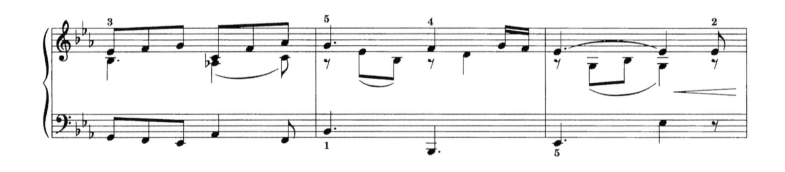

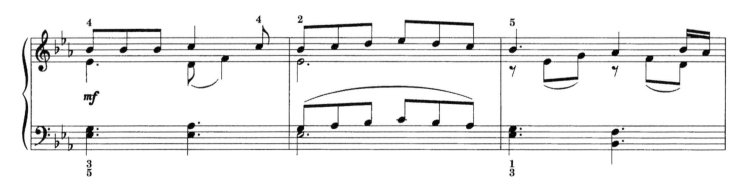

My Carmela
Carmela Mia

E. Cannio

Sextet from "Lucia di Lammermor"

Gaetano Donizetti

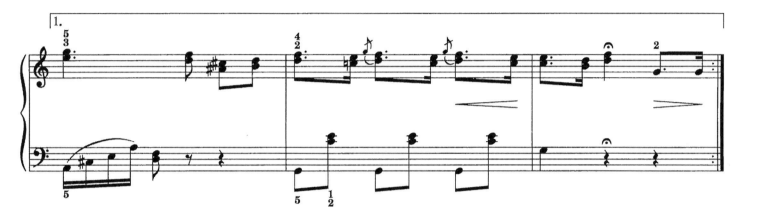

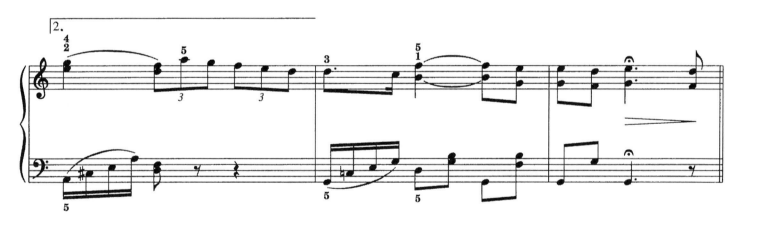

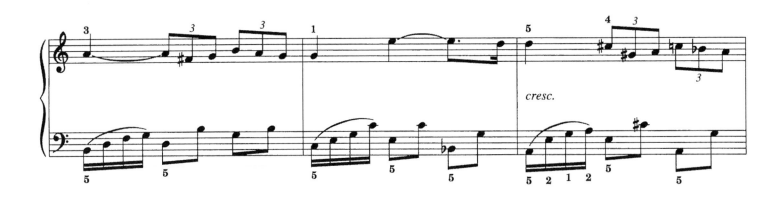

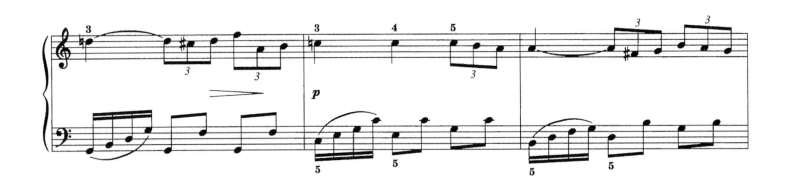

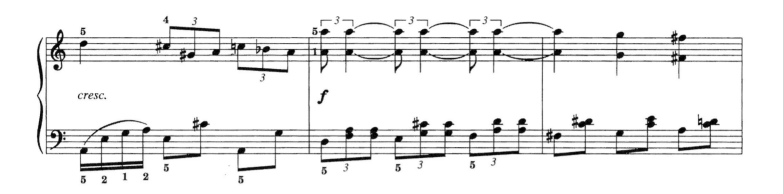

Il Bacio

Luigi Arditi

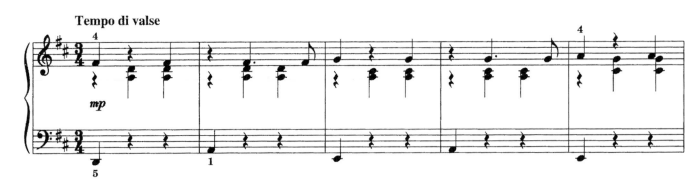

Parla

Eduardo di Capua

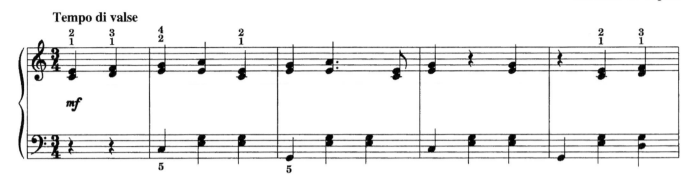

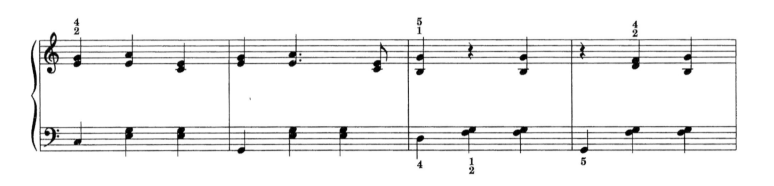

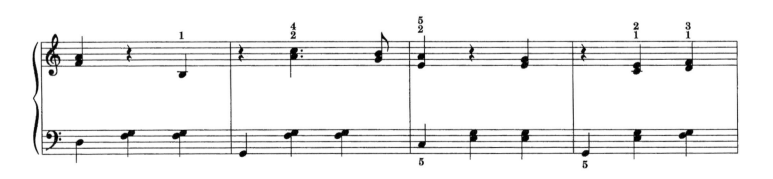

Carmé

G. B. de Curtis

Serenade of the Roses

Eduardo di Capua

Quartet from "Rigoletto"

Giuseppe Verdi

Mal Reggendo all' Aspro

from "Il Trovatore"

Giuseppe Verdi

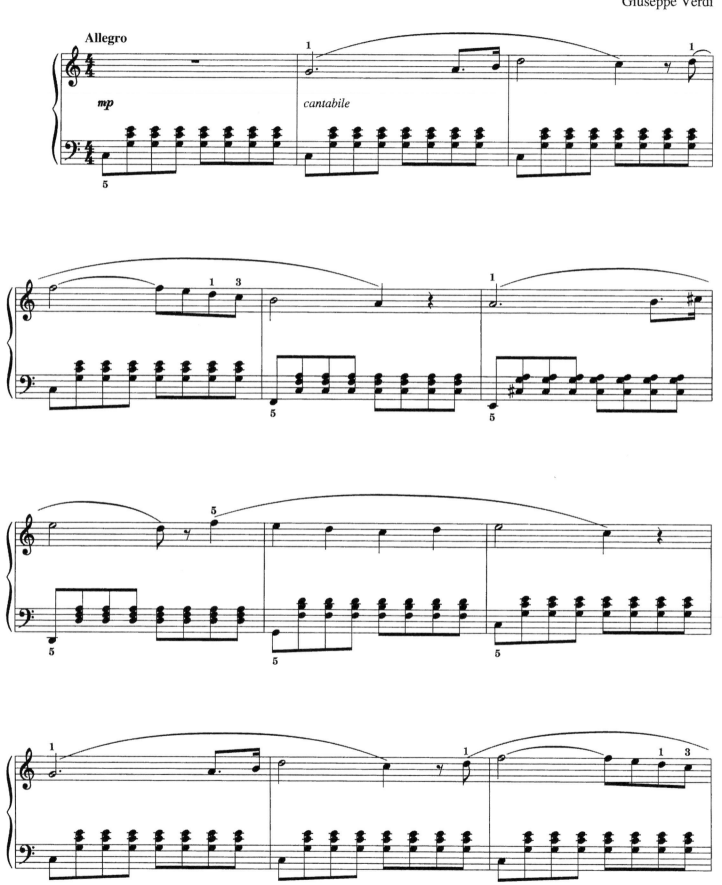

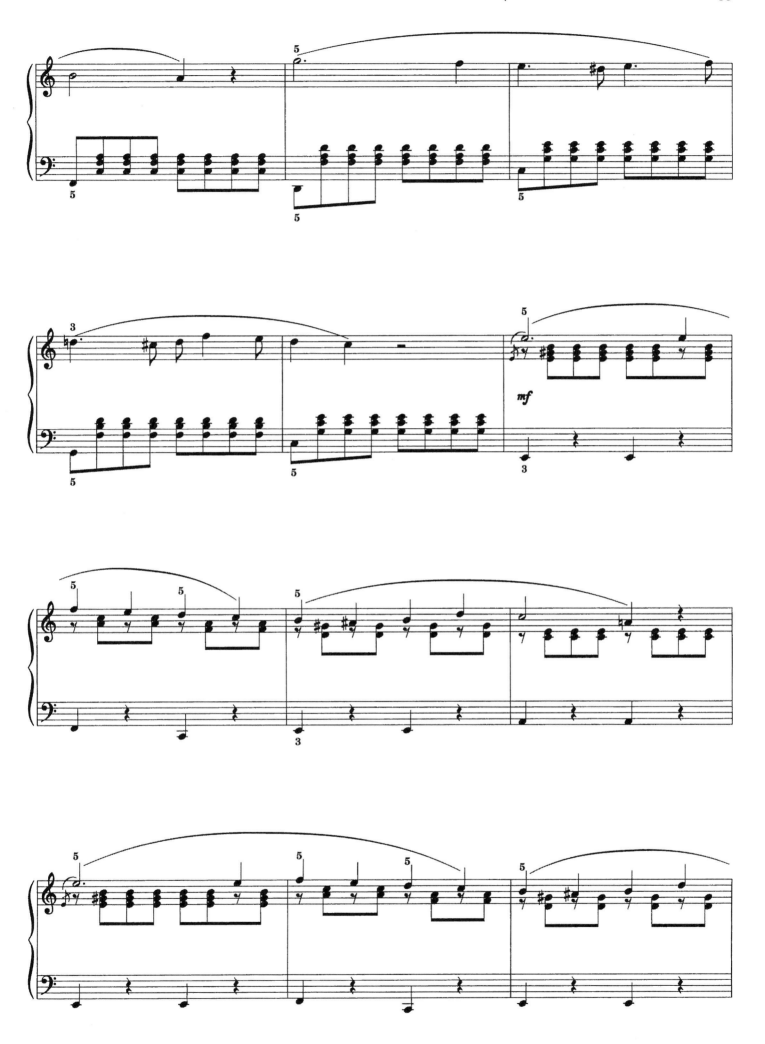

cresc. poco a poco

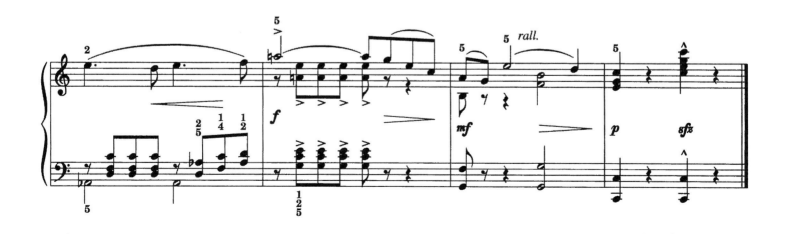

Una Furtiva Lagrima

from "L'Elisir d' Amore"

Gaetano Donizetti

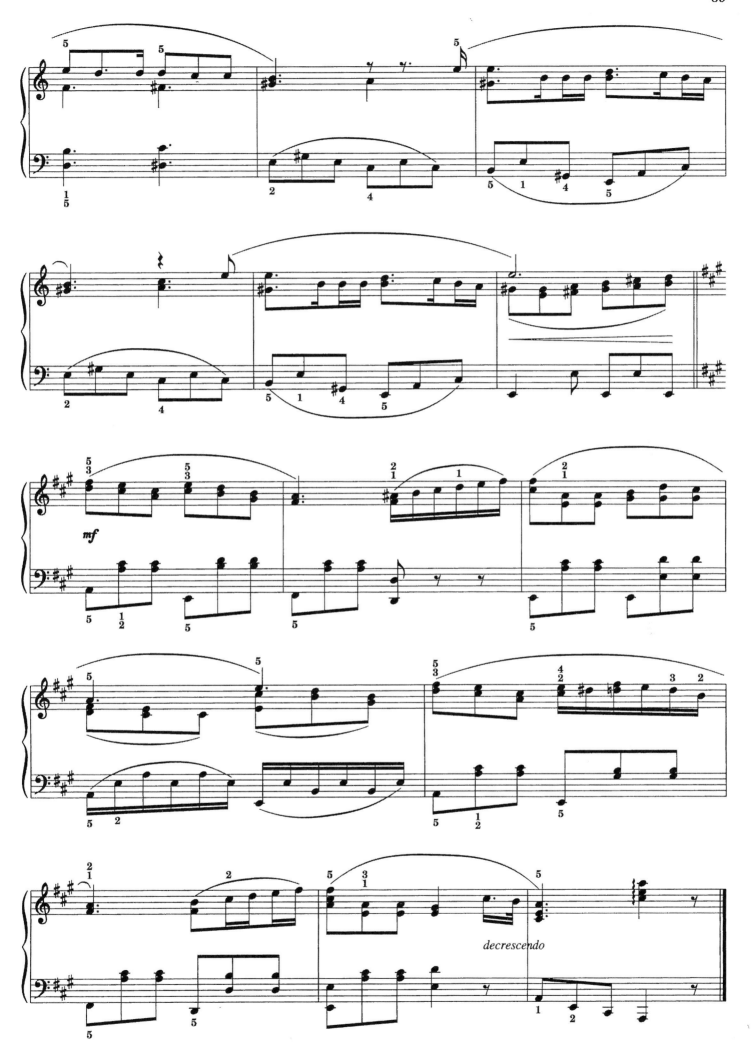

Goodbye to Naples
(L'Addio a Napoli)

Teodoro Cottrau

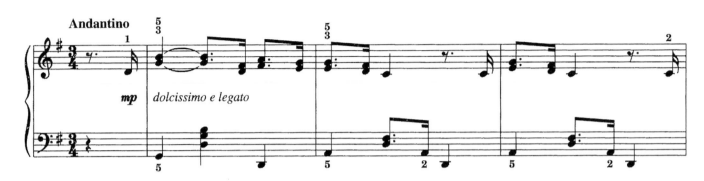

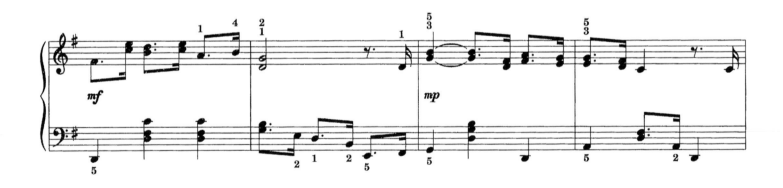

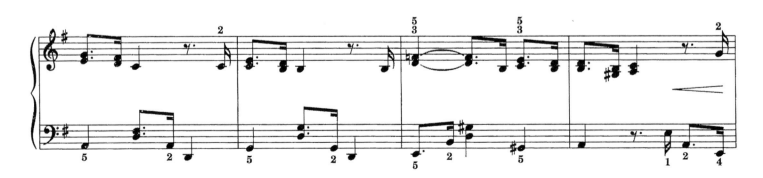

Doretta's Dream

from "La Rondine"

Giacomo Puccini

Sempre Libera

from "La Traviata"

Giuseppe Verdi

Brindisi (Drinking Song)

from "Cavalleria Rusticana"

Pietro Mascagni

Marie, Ah Marie

Eduardo di Capua

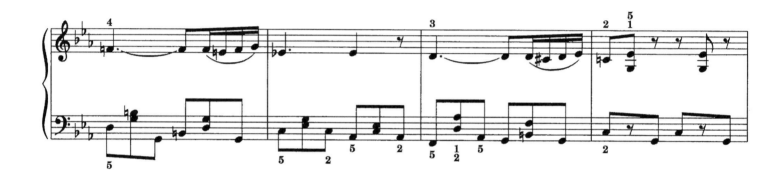

Questa o Quella

from "Rigoletto"

Giuseppe Verdi

I'Te Vurria Vasa

(Ah, Che Bel l'Aria Fresca)

Eduardo di Capua

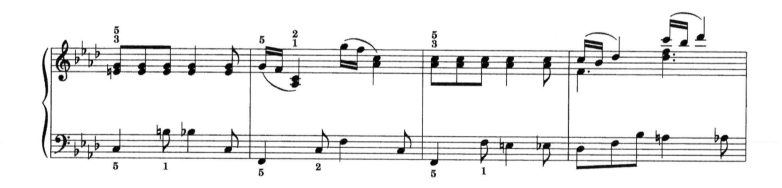

Serenata Napolitana

P. Mario Costa

Meno mosso

La Danza
(Tarantella)

Gioacchino Rossini

Allegro con brio